Date

Countries of the World

India

by Michael Dahl

Content Consultant:
Dr. R P Singh
Education Consulate
Embassy of India

Bridgestone Books

an imprint of Capstone Press

Bridgestone Books are published by Capstone Press
818 North Willow Street, Mankato, Minnesota 56001
http://www.capstone-press.com

Library of Congress Cataloging-in-Publication Data
Dahl, Michael S.
    India/by Michael Dahl.
    p. cm.--(Countries of the world)
    Includes bibliographical references and index.
    Summary: Discusses the history, landscape, people, animals, and culture
of the country of India.
    ISBN 1-56065-567-4
    1. India--Juvenile literature. [1. India.] I. Title.
II. Series: Countries of the world (Mankato, Minn.)
DS407.D28   1997
915.4--dc21
                                        97-5881
                                        CIP
                                        AC

Photo credits
Jean Buldain, 8
Michele Burgess, cover, 12, 14
Capstone Press, 5 (left)
Betty Crowell, 10
International Stock/Miwako Ikeda, 16
Unicorn Stock/Jim Shippee, 5 (right); N.G. Sharma, 6; Jean Higgins, 18;
    M. Amirtha, 20

Table of Contents

Fast Facts

Name: Republic of India
Capital: New Delhi
Population: More than 952 million
Language: Hindi
Religions: Hindu, Muslim

Size: 1,314,905 square miles
(3,418,753 square kilometers)
*India is less than one-third the size
of the United States.*
Crops: Rice, grain, sugar, spice, tea

Maps

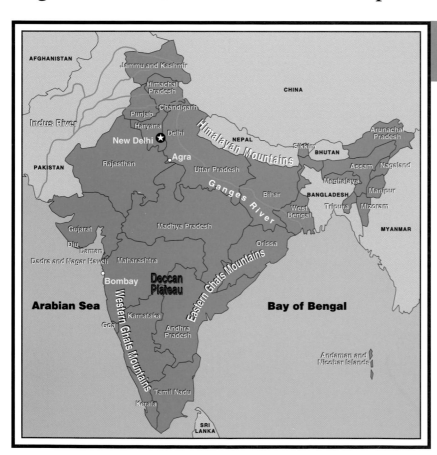

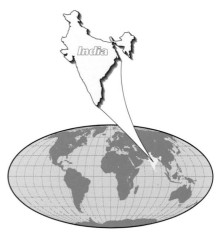

Flag

India's flag has three stripes. The top stripe is dark gold. The middle stripe is white. The bottom stripe is dark green. There is a blue wheel in the middle of the white stripe. It is Asoka's Wheel of Law. Long ago, Asoka ruled India. He led India into many wars. But then Asoka changed. He became peaceful. Asoka passed better laws. He wanted people to be peaceful and kind.

Currency

The rupee is the unit of currency in India.

It takes more than 34 rupees to equal one U.S. dollar.

The Land of India

India is the largest country in southern Asia. It is made up of 25 states and seven territories. A territory is land under the control of a nation.

India has the second largest population in the world. Population is the number of people who live somewhere. About 952 million people live in India. Only China has more people.

India also has many different religions. A religion is a set of beliefs people follow. Most Indians follow the Hindu or Muslim religions.

India is made up of many types of land. Its southern point reaches into the Indian Ocean. The northern part of India is covered by mountains. The Himalayas are the highest mountains in the world.

The Ganges and Indus rivers start in the Himalayas. India was named after the Indus River. Rivers are special in India. People honor rivers for giving them water.

The Himalayas are the world's highest mountains.

Going to School

In the past, many Indian children did not go to school. India is trying to fix that problem. India's government has built many new schools. School is free for students from age six to 14. Parents can also send their children to private schools. Private schools cost money.

Most city schools are like North American schools. The brick buildings have many classrooms. Each student sits at a desk. At many schools, students wear uniforms.

Schools in villages are different. Village schools usually do not have many classrooms. Sometimes they do not even have a building. Then classes are held outside.

India has more than 14 major languages. Hindi is the main language. Most Indian students learn three different languages. They learn Hindi and English. Most students usually learn Sanskrit, too. But sometimes they learn another language.

Sometimes village schools hold their classes outside.

9

At Home

There are different kinds of homes in India. Many Indians in cities live in houses and apartments. They have televisions and radios.

Houses are usually built with bricks and concrete. Most houses do not have basements. The houses do have flat roofs. The roofs have a ledge around them. Roofs with ledges are called terraces. Indian people enjoy spending time on their terraces. Sometimes they sleep there, too.

People in villages often build their own houses. These houses are made out of bricks and mud. Roofs are made of grasses.

Many village people put straw mats on their floors. They work and eat on these mats. Usually, a charpai is the only furniture in a village house. A charpai is a wooden bed. It has rows of rope instead of a mattress. In hot weather, some people move their charpais outside to sleep.

Sometimes people move their charpais outside.

Indian Clothing

India is a blend of old and new. Many people in India wear clothes like most North Americans. Some people still wear clothes from old times.

In villages, most men and boys wear dhotis (DOH-tees). A dhoti is a white strip of cotton. It is six feet (180 centimeters) long. A dhoti passes between the legs. Then it wraps around the upper legs and waist.

Women and girls wear colorful dresses called saris (SAH-rees). Some women and girls also wear a round dot on their foreheads. The dot is sometimes worn as a decoration. Other times it means that a women is married.

Pajamas are an Indian invention. Pajama is a Hindi word. It means clothing for the legs.

Many men wear turbans on their heads. A turban is a long piece of cloth wrapped around the head. Many women wear a colorful piece of cloth over their heads.

Many Indian people wear coverings on their heads.

Indian Food

Some Indians do not eat certain kinds of meat. Cows are special to the Hindu religion. Cows are kept safe because Hindus do not eat beef. Muslims do not eat pork. They consider pork unclean.

Most Indians like spicy vegetables and soup. Many northern Indians eat roti every day. Roti is round, flat bread. It is used to wrap around food. Many southern Indians eat rice with meals instead of roti.

Usually, family members gather together for meals. Food is served in small bowls or on banana leaves. Tea and coffee are favorite drinks.

Most Indian food is made with curry. Curry is a blend of strong spices. Meat and vegetables are cooked with it.

After meals, many Indians chew betel nuts and leaves. These nuts and leaves come from the betel palm tree. This helps calm upset stomachs. They also turn teeth and tongues a deep red.

Cows are kept safe because Hindus do not eat beef.

Animals in India

Most Indians practice the Hindu religion. Hindus believe that no living creatures should be hurt. Cows walk through the streets.

The Bengal (Ben-GAHL) tiger is the national animal of India. Most tigers are brown, orange, and black. Some Bengal tigers are white with black stripes. The Bengal is the largest tiger in the world.

Elephants also live in India. They help people do different jobs. Some elephants help lift heavy trees. They do this for Indian businesses that cut down trees. Businesses sell the trees for wood.

Elephants are painted and decorated for special parades. Long ago, Indian warriors rode elephants into battle. Warriors are brave fighters.

Elephants are painted and decorated for parades.

17

Indian Cities

New Delhi is the capital of India. Long ago, the rulers of India lived in New Delhi. They built many palaces and temples. Today, New Delhi is a modern and busy city. It still has many old buildings, too.

Agra is near New Delhi. The Taj Mahal was built in Agra. The Taj Mahal is a famous building. It was built by one of India's rulers. The building honored his dead wife.

Bombay is one of India's largest cities. Millions of people live there. Most Indian movies are made there. India makes more movies than any country in the world.

All Indian cities have special things to see and do. Animals and people live side by side in Indian cities. Horses pull buggies. Different kinds of birds sit on buildings. Cows walk through alleys.

The Taj Mahal is a famous building in Agra, India.

Indian Holidays

There are about 50 Hindu holidays in India. These holidays honor gods, goddesses, and heroes. People have camel and boat races on some holidays. There are also elephant parades and puppet shows.

Diwali (duh-WAH-lee) is the most important Hindu holiday. It honors the goddess Lakshmi (LOCK-schmee). Lakshmi is the goddess of wealth and beauty.

Diwali is also the Hindu New Year. Fireworks light up the sky in every city. People dress up in new clothes and give presents.

In the spring, Indians have Color Day. People wear old clothes on this day. Indians sprinkle friends and strangers with shiny powder. They squirt each other with colored water. Everyone ends up wet and colorful.

People race boats during some holidays.

Hands On: Play Kabaddi

Kabaddi (kah-BAH-dee) is a popular Indian running game. Many people can play it.

What You Need

Four or more players
A large playing area

What You Do

1. Divide the players into two equal teams. Each team picks one side of the playing area. One team starts. They pick a player to run onto the other team's side.
2. The runner takes a deep breath. The runner tries to tag the other team's players. The runner must tag people without taking another breath. The runner must keep saying "kabaddi-kabaddi." This way the runner cannot take another breath.
3. The other players try to keep from getting tagged. Those who have been tagged try to catch the runner. They try to keep the runner on their side.
4. The runner must run back to his or her own side without taking another breath. Then all the players who were tagged are out. Otherwise, the runner is out.
5. The teams take turns until everyone has been the runner.
6. The team with the most players still in the game wins.

Learn to Speak Hindi

beautiful	sundar	(soon-DAR)
father	pita	(PIT-ah)
good-bye and hello	namastay	(nah-MAH-stay)
how are you?	kya hal hai	(key-AH HAHL HI)
hurry up	jaldi karo	(jahl-DEE kah-ROH)
mother	mata	(MAH-tah)
no	nahi	(NAH-hee)
thank you	dhanyavad	(don-YAH-vahd)
yes	haan	(HAI IN)

Words to Know

charpai (CHAHR-pay)—a wooden bed with rows of rope instead of a mattress

curry (KUH-ree)—a powder made of different spices

dhoti (DOH-tee)—a long strip of cotton that is wrapped around the upper legs and waist

Lakshmi (LOCK-schmee)—the Hindu goddess of wealth and beauty

sari (SAH-ree)—a long piece of cloth that is wrapped around a woman's body

terrace (TER-iss)—a flat roof with a ledge around it

territory (TER-uh-tor-ee)—a large area of land

Read More

Haskins, Jim. *Count Your Way Through India*. Minneapolis: Carolrhoda Books, 1990.

Kalman, Bobbie. *India, the Culture*. New York: Crabtree Publishing Company, 1990.

Useful Addresses and Internet Sites

Asia Studies Association
University of Michigan
Ann Arbor, MI 48109

Embassy of India
2107 Massachusetts Avenue NW
Washington, DC 20008

Government of India
http://www.meadev.gov.in

India Net
http://www.india-net.com

Index